Finally
I Listened
And
I Heard Him Say...

NATHALIA EQUIHUA

WESTBOW
PRESS®
A DIVISION OF THOMAS NELSON
& ZONDERVAN

Scripture taken from the New King James Version. Copyright 1979, 1980, 1982 by Thomas Nelson, inc. Used by permission. All rights reserved.

WestBow Press books may be ordered through booksellers or by contacting:

WestBow Press
A Division of Thomas Nelson & Zondervan
1663 Liberty Drive
Bloomington, IN 47403
www.westbowpress.com
1 (866) 928-1240

Because of the dynamic nature of the Internet, any web addresses or links contained in this book may have changed since publication and may no longer be valid. The views expressed in this work are solely those of the author and do not necessarily reflect the views of the publisher, and the publisher hereby disclaims any responsibility for them.

Any people depicted in stock imagery provided by Thinkstock are models, and such images are being used for illustrative purposes only. Certain stock imagery © Thinkstock.

ISBN: 978-1-4908-3887-8 (sc)
ISBN: 978-1-4908-3886-1 (hc)
ISBN: 978-1-4908-3888-5 (e)

Library of Congress Control Number: 2014909662

Print information available on the last page.

WestBow Press rev. date: 11/06/2018

03/02/83

My daughter listen to Me and record the words that I say.

04/23/83

Listen to Me My daughter. Record all that I am about to say.

02/26/86

My Beloved daughter do not be afraid to write the words that you hear for they cometh from your heart and what cometh from your heart cometh from Me.

05/25/86

My daughter why do you hesitate to write My word? Do you not, after all I have given you, trust what you hear in your heart? I speak these words to your heart not just for others, but for yourself also.

02/24/98

You have written as I have spoken to you.

11/11/98

My little one it has been awhile since I last called you to record My words.

To my brothers and sisters in Christ,

The Lord has spoken to my heart many times. I can't remember the exact date of when I first heard Him. Neither can I recall when He first told me to record what I heard. I found the words on the previous page in personal messages from Him. Those messages are not included in these writings. I will share those words with you at a later date. I do remember offering some resistance when awaken in the middle of the night. I would suggest to the Lord that He just tell me His message and I would record it in the morning. What a brat I was. Well I finally got over that. Please read His words. Listen to them with your heart. Share them with everyone. He is speaking to all of us.

Nathalia

11/03/81 (2:50 a.m.)

Are you really and truly looking for gifts to bring to Me on Christmas? Do you really and truly want to do something special for Me during this season? Then My child put these thoughts into your heart. My list includes your burdens, your anxieties, your sick, your poor in spirit, your anger, your pain, your persecuted, and most of all your heart. These are the gifts that I look forward to seeing at the foot of the cross. For you have heard me say "Come to Me all those who are burdened and I will give you rest." You cannot rest when you carry a load heavier than yourself. Yes, I have told you to care for the sick, feed My flock, and you must be able to carry your cross as I did. But you have over looked the most important part. That is you must do these things under the power of the Holy Spirit. That is lovingly with His joy and peace. It is only by giving Me your open heart that I can walk right in and give you rest – a state of rest that the world knows not. Give all to Me so that I may give all to you. For it is when you give freely that you receive freely. You cannot of your own will love My sick, poor, aged, every ethnic; but through the power of God our Father. The Holy Spirit will love all for you. You can also embrace the leper and you can truly love yourself. Did you know that you are not truly loving yourself when you have not given Me your heart? All of your words of love are merely lip service, things of the mind, and surface words. But when you have opened your heart to Me, then you will begin to know love as the Father loves. I love you. I love you. I love you many more times than the steps you have taken in your life. Count them and you will begin to know how much I and the Father love you. Come bearing these gifts My child.

11/13/81 (2:00 a.m.)

My children, My children, My children, how long I have waited for your love. I love you. I love you deeply. There are no words on earth to express how much I love you. And yet, you have shut Me out of your heart, I the creator of all – yes, even your heart. Open it so that you may know Me fully. Read the book of Acts, especially chapter 14. See what I can give to you. Know that I have so much to give. I love to give, but you tell Me no! You say there is no room. There is no time, I have you altogether in my head, and do not bother with my heart. Why have you shut Me out? What do you fear? Is it losing your own will? What have you gained through your own will? Is it knowledge? Is there not another wiser than you? Is it beauty? Is there not another more beautiful than you? Is it fame or popularity? Isn't there always one more popular than you? Take all that you have gained from this world and hold it in your hands. Look at it. Does it love you? Does it comfort you? Does it give you peace deep within your heart? Oh, how worthless are these earthly treasures. How they can be crumbled to pieces. But not the treasures that My Father has stored for you. Unclutter your mind and heart with all of these vain desires. Empty yourselves -- now wait -- not as long as I have waited for you, but a short while. Wait in the quiet stillness of your heart and hear Me coming. Your heart beats with a new rhythm. It says, I love you, I love you, I love you. And as you feel and receive My love for you, begin to love and reach out to others. Be still and receive My peace -- now give it away. Receive My strength -- now give it away. Oh, how I long to give these things and so much more; if you would just open your heart and empty your will and receive. Reach out for the most precious gift of all, LOVE. Without it, all else is lost! I Love you!

11/22/81 (1:00 a.m.)

Teens of today hear what I say. I know that on this day you have prayed that I have heard the message from your heart. Know without a doubt that all things, those you wish Me to know and those you rather not known are known unto Me as clear as a bell. Your heart does tell whether in My hands you made your plans. Do you wonder how I know? So many times I've told you so. I live at your hearts front door. Won't you open it and let Me in? All I want is to be your friend. To get you through lifes great rush is not enough, but to enter your heart is a must. I'll wait as long as you want Me to. Yes, even until you're old and gray. But if you can find a way, won't you let it happen today? Oh My child you must know how in My heart I've loved you so. I've loved you through your mother. I've loved you through your father. I've loved you through a friend. I have loved you again and again and again. Why is it just the pain you see instead of the love given by Me? There are many closed doors that you are yet to see. But, if you come by Me then all you will see. You will seek and you shall find. You will ask and it shall be given. Yes you will knock and the doors (even those close doors) shall be opened up to you. So My children put your trust in Me and then you will see a glorious new day full of peace from heaven. I love you so. I cannot say it enough. It's with every breath you take even that's lesser. I have for you a poem to say.

> **I open my heart to Jesus as He**
> **comes to me this day.**
> **I know He'll love me tender, as**
> **my heart I do surrender.**
> **I will not fear to do as I hear, for**
> **I know He's always near.**

Keep these words in your heart and love one another. I love you My children. Come unto Me.

12/03/81 (3:15 a.m.)

My people, My children, hear what I say. I am in this world this day and every day. I have not forsaken you. I will not leave you orphaned. I love you much too much to desert you. I watch over you. I protect you from the hailstones. I love you when you think you are not being loved. I provide for you when you think there will be no provisions. Why do you think that you walk alone? Is it because you cannot see Me or touch Me? Do you not believe that there is a heart within your body that sustains your life? Can you see it or touch it? No, you only hear it. And it is so with Me. Though you cannot see or touch Me, I am so very real, more than real in your life. Be still and you can hear Me too as you hear your heartbeat. I, more than your heart, sustain your life. I love you. Why do you think you are strong enough to be here at this very moment? Did you not have one exhausting day and yet you have heard Me call and you have come. For this you shall reap a fountain of new strength and total peace in all of your trials, for I love you. You are My good and faithful servant. I find much joy in you. Spend much time in stillness and listen for My voice. I speak to you many times, but you find ways to drown Me out. Again, just as you can only hear or detect the sound of your heartbeat in total silence – so it is with My voice. I am with you. Do not be afraid to hear Me. I love you. I only come to prepare you to see and meet My Father face to face. He waits for you. And oh what joy He has when His sheep hear and obey. So that you will know that I am with you, I surround you with My cloud of peace now at this very moment. A peace you have never known. I want you to soak it in. Be still in it and I will anoint you with the Holy Spirit. Do not be afraid to speak what you hear in this peace. For each one will hear much. Whether you hear words that man speaks or foreign tongues, believe Me you will hear. Do not fear what others will say or think for all will hear. Why is anyone here if it is not to hear My voice and My Father's promises? Listen above the sounds of the room. Receive your gifts of tongue, interpretation, wisdom, prophecy, and healing. I am with you to give you life more abundantly. Please accept My gifts. I love you.

01/01/82 (1:45 a.m.)

Listen My children to the ways in which you are to live this New Year. Are not the words familiar? You shall not bear false witnesses. You shall not covet thy neighbor's wife. You shall love thy neighbor as thyself, as thyself, as thyself! When My children will you learn to love yourself as I love you? Do you not know where your pain comes from? It is not from others, but it is merely because you are not loving yourself. When you truly love yourself as I love you or in other words, allow Me to love you through you, no other can cause you pain. If they, others, give pain it returns to them. If they, others, give love it is received and they are loved in return. Can you not see My children that love is a perfect circle? There is no beginning with man and no end with man. All love is from God the Father. Open your heart to Him, the creator of all, and allow Him to love you and others through you. It is then that you will see the beauty in yourself reflected in those around. You are beautiful. You are handsome. The Father has carved you from the palm of His hand. His hand not the hand of some ungodly creature, but His very own hand. Accept this truth. Know in your heart that you are His child and that He wants His good for you. Snuggle close to Him. He does not want to be a statue that you worship, but a loving, protective, providing Father. Let it be. Let His will be done in you as it is written in heaven.

01/11/82 (3:40 a.m.)

My people, how long I have waited for your love and shall continue to wait and wait until you finally decide to take Me from the pages of a book, from the plaques on the wall, from the statues on the shelf and put Me tenderly in your hearts. You are the only one that can do this. How will you know when you have put Me into your heart? When you love your brothers and sisters as I love you. My heart grows sad with the coldness of your heart. You have become like the plastic flower. You look like My people, but there is no warmth, no sweetness. Have you not read My word? Greet one another with a Holy kiss. Not a duty kiss within the walls of a building, but the love and tenderness that I, the Father gives to you anytime, anywhere, whenever, wherever, FOREVER. You sing – "They'll know we are Christians by our Love". Do you love? Oh My people, do you not know that you must have Me in your heart to love as I love. Come away from the world of formalities. Do not perform duties for Me. Love for Me. Allow Me to love through you. I love you so very deeply. I pain for you so very deeply. Be not afraid to be still and go within yourself and find the true beauty I have created you to be. Just as a rose is a beauty to behold, are you not the same? Did I not create you to be over all things on the earth, not just ruler but in beauty too. Why do you wish to remain a plastic people? Come aside and listen to and behold with your eyes all that your senses respond to. It's the same coldness that I feel from your heart. Please, please don't continue to freeze Me out. Let Me in to warm your heart and allow the tender loving beauty within to blossom for others to behold. And then and only then can you sing, "They'll know We Are Christians By Our Love".

01/24/82 (6:40 a.m.)

My people, My precious little people. Why have you not heard My call? So many times through so many deliveries I have said love one another, share with one another and yet only a small number of you have responded. Have you not heard that not all that call Lord Lord will enter the gates of heaven? Have you not heard that many only offer lip service? Have you not heard that you must carry Me in your heart? Have you not heard that there is none worst than a luke warm heart? I can't accept your refusal to hear what is said. Oh My people, such a hardened people. If you have heard My word in your heart, then speak out and save your brothers and sisters. Pray with and for them. For when you have truly listened in your heart then you silently mourn for them for they are dying within. So speak of what you hear in your heart to melt the ice and turn their hearts into the same burning fire of love and hunger that you carry. As an expecting mother beams with joy as she feels her unborn within her womb, then all should jump for joy and rejoice and praise and sing alleluia with the newborn Christ in their hearts. Remove the starch from their collars. Put blinders on their eyes. Erase the words from their heads. Fill them with the joy in your heart. Love them tenderly, love them now. Allow none to leave empty for all have been called.

02/23/82 (12:01 a.m.)

My people listen to these concerns of yours. What shall I give up or sacrifice for this season? What shall I do special for this season? What will the Lord do for me this season? How shall I pray this season? Why? Why do you bother to ask yourself these questions when neither of them are the key to really knowing Me. How shall you eat, with a hunger for My Word and My Love. What will I give you? Eternal everlasting life, life more abundantly, joy during trials, peace in times of trouble, and love unlimited. You need not concern yourself with any set formula or rules. All you need do is know My Word in your heart and let My Will be done. My Will is to walk with you in happy times, carry you through troubled waters, and to give to you until your cup runneth over with love for one another. Are you really and truly ready and fully prepared to walk with Me these 40 days? Do you know what you're in for? Death! Do you know that your desires for worldly things will die? Do you know that you will no longer be in charge of your life? Do you know that you will rise, yes be born again to serve Me and to feed My flock? This is the road to Calvary. Is this why you have come to follow this path? If so say yes Lord over and over in your heart and I will prepare the way for you, the way to eternal life. I love you and I wait for you.

06/13/82 (2:25 a.m.)

While attending a spiritual conference for women, I gave a prophecy in which our Lord spoke of His love for us. His words were that He loves us even in our sin. The leader acknowledged that the words that I spoke were from the Lord, but said that God does not love you when we sin. Shortly after I got home our Lord told me to write the prophecy on the next page.

6/13/82 (2:25 a.m.)

Women of the world, is not your faith built upon My word? Is not My word spoken and recorded by many prophets? Have you not accepted the words written in My Holy Scripture? Where have you found that I, the Father of all creation does not love the sinner? Did you not come to Me as a sinner soiled and tattered and worn out by the ways of the world? Did I not accept you with open arms, heal and caress your every pain? How can you speak the words that I have not loved you in your sin? Do you think that you, created from dust as all mankind, are free from sin at this moment now? No My child. For you have not been made aware of all your sinful ways. Forget not that I am the Father and that all things are known unto Me. I am with you when you have torn your neighbor apart with words as well as when you praise Me. I am with you when you have passed judgment on My other children as well as when you call upon Me. I am with you when you lied so as to have your way as well as when you have asked for forgiveness. I am with you when you have boasted and have been swollen up over others as well as when you have danced for Me. I am with you when you have had sinful desires in your heart as when you shout glory. I am with you when your faith has grown faint, almost disappeared, as well as when you trust totally in My word. Oh My child forget not that I am the Father and that all things spoken and within the deepest part of your mind and heart are known unto Me. I look beyond your faults. I look beyond your sin. I tally your goodness and yes My child I love all of you, every atom in your body. Never lacking a second I am there always loving you. How can you doubt that I do not love you in your sinfulness? How else do you come to Me? Not one of My children have been instantly cleansed of all of his sinfulness. You come to Me a step at a time. Each step on My path is a step out of the world. Yes My child you have come a long way and I shall continue to draw you ever so close until you know Me fully. Seek Me with all of your heart. Spend as much time with Me alone as you do with your community of love. For I have many things to say to you. Oh yes I am always whispering of My love for you. Many times you turn away because you have sinned and think that I will not love you. But oh My child the love that I have for you is greater than any love you have ever known. My love for you can never be comprehended by man. It is greater than all creation on the earth. Yes My child I love you in your purity and in your sinfulness. I love you always. Think not that the intellect knoweth all things. Continue to read My word. Listen to and accept those words written and spoken by My prophets. Listen to My words spoken from your heart and not those reasoned out by the intellect of the mind. I love you and though you have taken many steps into your heavenly home, not the most holiest of man has reached the door. Seek Me with all of your heart. For it is in seeking Me that your sins are washed away. Seek Me and I will draw you closer revealing more unto you, pouring gifts upon you, and cleansing you step by step. I love you My child. I've loved you always. I'll love you forever.

07/09/82 (3:28 a.m.)

My children it is My heart's desire to set your souls on fire. The fire of a burning love to nurture every heart near to you and afar. My love is like that you've never known. My love heals. My love forgives. My love is compassionate. My love believes. My love is wise. My love is warm. My love is all -- all that there is on earth and above. It can be seen all around you. It can be felt within you. My love is real. It is everlasting. There is no beginning or end for My love. It always has been and it always will be. Have you known anything of this earth that is the same? Listen, My children I know of the fears in your heart. I know of the things that you have listened to about the gifts that I have for you and of those that call Me into their heart. Be not afraid My child. You are precious to Me. I know what is in your heart; the desires -- all of them, and the tears -- all of them, and the fears -- all of them. I would never step without your approval.

But oh how I want that approval. Your approval to heal the scars upon your heart. Your approval to set fire to your very soul so that you may be a light to all around. So that you may touch your family, your friends, all of your love ones just with your light. Your light My child brings each one around you to the perfect light -- Jesus Christ. Feel the love of Christ around you. Feel the love of Christ within you. Know that the burning in your heart is the love of Christ within you. Yes My child the Holy Spirit is upon you. The Holy Spirit is love. Are you willing to be My light? Are you willing to be My burning flame of love? Then seek not this or that gift. Think not that this or that one is better or more important than the other. But know that as you accept My Holy Spirit you accept the oneness that is. It is in this oneness that you begin to function as part of the body, the body of Christ. I love you. I love each member of My body. It is for the body to desire the love that keeps it alive, that causes it to heal, that causes it to listen to the Father. Love is the key to all things on earth and above. Love My children. Love one another as one and each one. I love you. I love you. Accept My love.

08/02/82 (2:31 a.m.)

Listen My children you have been called from far and near to hear the words which you should carry to the children I love so dear. Each of you a vessel of which I have chosen to bear fruit and spread seeds among those you come from. Do not fear how it will be done for I will lead the way. Be still with Me often to find the light of each day. Come to Me My child and see what I have to offer – a land of peace and honey until My final coming. Did you not know that you are here by My will and not that of your own? Yes, I have called you to be My very own messenger of deliverance from sin and shame. Why do you concern yourselves with what you should say and how it should be said and with what you should do and how it should be done? Did you not know that I have prepared you to care for all those that I send your way? This is a time of stillness to hear My word each day allowing it to saturate your soul showing you the way.

The way to peace and harmony for others sent your way. Just be still My child and set your mind on Me not on formulas or on decrees of efficiency. My love—yes—My love is sufficient for all graces received, this you shall see. I love you My children each and all of you. I have called you here to shepherd my flock to eternity. Listen with your heart. I love you.

12/12/83 (3:00 a.m.)

I am among many strangers whose home they call my own. My Father speaks and out they sneak to follow a mind of their own. My name they do proclaim as they seek their personal fame. My children cry what a shame as they mar and disgrace My name. Have you ever stopped to think what a blessing a pure heart can gain? When with a pure heart My name you proclaim, a stranger you are no more for you've truly opened the door. Your love will grow I know as I dwell there for evermore. So do not stay a stranger with a heart as dark as night, for I am your friend Jesus. I can make you My pure bright light. Remove your mask for others. You all have hurts to share. Pray for one another as My love you will share. Sharing My body makes us one as My body you become and a new life you've begun. Know that I love you My children. Remove Me from the throne in your head and cradle Me in your heart. Come Lord

Jesus, come Lord Jesus is the song you should sing with opened arms to let Me walk right in. When you know that in your heart I'm in then close your arms around Me and let Me love you My friend.

11/12/84 (time unknown)

My children, how I long to hold you tenderly in My arms with your complete trust of My Fatherhood. I am your Father. I am the one true Father of all. You are My children. I care for each of you individually. It is I that provides for you. It is I that carries you when you are weak. It is I that caresses you when you are lonely. I am always with you. I am always in full knowledge of your needs. I long to fulfill each of them. All I need is your trust. How often have you not seen the way and yet those times have passed ever so swiftly? How often have you wondered how and found the answer before you? Know that I am always providing for you. The more you trust in My provisions, the more peace and joy you will have. Trust Me for your daily bread. Trust Me with your love ones. Trust Me with time itself, for I alone know the appointed time for all things. I love you My children. I love you. Nothing can ever remove My love for you. Please accept it and surrender all things unto Me. I am your Father.

11/24/84 (time unknown)

My children how I long for you to come and rest with Me awhile. I need the quiet stillness of all creation in order to speak to your hearts. There is so much that I have to say— so much that you need to hear for peace of heart, mind, and soul. I have called you before this time and you have heard Me, but always you choose a way to busy yourselves. I need the oneness of couples and single heartedness of singles. All have been called. I am your Father. Can you not hear Me? Do you not know that you are to respond to My request? How I long to spend this time alone with you. Come My children, there is much for us to do. This is a time to kindle the sparks that I have given you, a time to fill your hearts with My unlimited love, a time of healing the many wounds of your hearts, a time for blossoming flowers of gifts deeply rooted. Come and allow Me to caress you. You are My children. I am your father. Do not turn away from Me. I love you. I love you. I love you.

12/27/87 (time unknown)

The words that I give unto you are not for the world, but those who are not of the world. Let them know of My love. I know that they are tired as you are tired. I know that they long to come home as you long to come home. I know that they have been mocked and rejected in many ways. I need for My precious children to know that My promises will be fulfilled. Satan will not stand victorious over My little ones—My flock. They must continue (as you must) continue to persevere. They must hold on to the promises that I have given each of them. They must love one another passionately. They must not become luke warm. That is a fate worse than Satan himself. Be on fire with My word and My love. Be on fire with songs of praise and My love. Be on fire with compassion and My love, My love, My love. My love is what is to be poured out from each one of My little ones, My flock. Do not become complacent with the ways of the world. They must come fully into the kingdom. Pray together and for one another. Come aside and hear Me speak to each heart alone. For I love each precious one even more and with greater passion as My entire flock. Do not hold on to your injuries, but rather pour them out before Me and leave them with Me. Most of all they are to know that they are never, never alone. Always I am with each one of My children. In the darkest of night I am there. Not standing in a corner watching, but there holding each one in My arms in stillness, walking hand in hand, sharing each day, and carrying each one over troubled water. Which one of you would see your own child suffer and not do all you can to remove the cause of the suffering? So it is even more so with Me. I see and knoweth all things. I alone knoweth how much each heart can bear. I alone can strengthen each heart through the power of the Holy Spirit. Never give up hope. For man knows not the appointed time nor the number of days given to each one. But live each day to the fullest according to God's will. Believing that if not this day or the next—on the right day His will—will be done. Wash your hands completely of the ways of the world. Stand fully in the grace of God. Know, receive, and give My love. This is My deepest desire. I love you—each one of you.

04/02/11 (12:15 a.m.)

Do not allow sorrow to create anger and depression for I the Lord thy God have brought you out of darkness into light. I have prepared a table before you with all of your needs. Feast upon the peace and joy. Take as many healings as you need. Embrace those gifts. Make a joyful noise unto the Lord. Keep your eyes on the Lord. Do not turn back to darkness. There are many evil spirits waiting for you. My sheep recognize and follow one voice, the Shepherd, My voice.

04/03/11 (2:30 a.m.)

My children I hear your cries in the night. The cries come from the depth of your heart. Be not afraid for I am with you. I will not forsake you. Reach out to Me and I will hold your hand and send forth My peace that surpasses all mankind. Do not worry as to whether you should do this or that or say this or that. Know that I the Father will lead you on the path that you should follow. You will be led by My wisdom, if that is what you have chosen. There is peace for all of those that choose to let go of whatever they wrestle with. Can you imagine? No worry! Come My little ones, surrender all to Me. Stay awhile in the psalm of My hand. Rest in Peace. All things will come in their due season. Trust Me. Call upon Me. Rest in Me. I am your Father. I AM.

04/05/11 (time unknown)

Why have so many gone astray? Are you not listening to the words that you read from My Bible? Come sit before My throne and listen to your Heavenly Father. I knew you before you were in your mother's womb. I protected your development and taught you only good. When you were born you began to hear other voices. You knew they were not My voice. You learned from those other voices some good some bad. My voice seemed to fade away, but it is there. I will never leave you and My voice speaks to you forever. Perhaps you cannot hear Me because of anger, jealousy, unforgiveness, or even false idols. As you know I am the beginning and the end. All things are provided for those that seek Me and trust Me. I'm always with you. Perhaps you cannot hear Me because of the spirits sent by Satan. Rebuke them in Jesus name. Beware that they don't return. Now when all evil is rebuked, come and soak in My Holy Spirit and listen. Come to your Heavenly Father and listen.

04/09/11 (1:00 a.m.)

Many have called upon Me and I have answered, but few listen to My answer. If you think I have not answered, then read My word. The answer will be the same. All seek love, peace, joy, healing, and wisdom; but they do not open themselves to receive these things. All you need do is say yes Lord. I am always trying to give you what you seek but you have not made time to accept these gifts. Come My children. Come and bath in the light of the Lord. Deny all things that hold you back. Come into your Father's house. I love you. I love you. Do not be afraid nor anxious about anything for I am with you. Put your hand in mine. Trust Me. Lay your burdens down and do not pick them up again. Use My light to move through darkness. Love one another and sit in silence and hear My voice. I AM.

04/12/11 (2:10 a.m.)

My children listen to your Heavenly Father. So many times I have called you to walk with Me and you turned a deaf ear while I listened to your heart of the many things you desire. Do you not know that you must seek the kingdom of God first with all of your heart, your mind, your soul, and your strength? I have come again and again and knocked at the door of your heart. But you are too busy trying to obtain your heart's desire. Those are things you will obtain (if they be in My will) as you seek Me. As you seek Me many of the things that you thought you wanted will be forgotten. And you will want more and more of Me. You will receive the peace that surpasses all understanding, love, joy, and wisdom. So you need not worry about when you will get this or that. For all things come in their season. And only the Father knows the season for everything in heaven and earth. Pray unceasingly! I AM.

06/25/11 (11:31 p.m.)

Pray as I have instructed you to do. Remember, seek ye first the kingdom of God and all things will come unto you. Pray, praise, and glorify Me, the Heavenly Father, and Jesus Christ, My only Son and the Holy Spirit in all you do. With all these things in mind knock and the door shall open. Ask and it shall be given. Seek and ye shall find. You each have a great hunger for My word and ye shall be fed. You also thirst and that thirst shall continuously be quenched. Believe that you can never get enough of My word. Absorb what you have read and now seek and invite My Holy Spirit to enter your heart. He will lead you, encourage you, and fill you with all you need to be a light to My perfect light. Know that I am with you. I will come to you alone, but if you need more encouragement I will give you a light to follow. Surely you will follow the light that I send. You are so special to Me. I await to see your beautiful painted wings. I love you! I AM.

07/26/11 (time unknown)

My little ones: You need not ever worry or be concerned about your daily bread. Yes it is true that those words or that request is spoken in the words that I have given you to pray, but you speak knowing that you will receive from Me. You need not fear the problems of the world. Many have taken much more than their portion and left others to starve. This is not the way it is written in scripture. Many turn their back on those in need as they count their huge sums. Pray My little ones, for it will not be long before the chosen ones will harvest much. Those that hide treasure from others shall reap no more. They will find that what they have hidden has become worthless. My sheep heard My voice and followed it. Great is their reward, both on earth and in heaven. Praise the Lord. Thank the Lord. Trust the

Lord. Listen for Him and follow Him always. For in Him there is NO wrong. Follow Him and receive His love, peace, joy and wisdom now and forever. Believe that I AM.

08/23/11 (time unknown)

My Children how I long to walk with and talk to each one of you. This is possible you know. The Lord your God is omnipresent which means that I can be in more than one place at the same time. I am with you giving you all of My love and attention and at the same time I am with many of My other children. What do I want of you? I want you to hunger and thirst for My word. And after you have filled yourself with My written word you can share the words written (both in the Bible and prophecy). Share God's word with as many as I send to you. Surely you will begin to weaken, so refuel with My words again so that they can energize you. There are so many stiff necks in the church. Show them My love. It is warm, caring, healing, joyful, and unconditional. It truly doesn't get any better than this because it comes from I Am directly through you to others. Continue to pray and read My words. I love you. I give you peace. Listen to Me.

09/12/11 (3:00 a.m.)

My beloved children do you not hear Me calling your name? Yes, I have called all of My children together now. But there are times when I have called each of you by name to spend some time with Me. Are you too busy to give Me a few moments alone so that I can fill you with all that you need to do what I have called you to do? When you hear Me calling harden not your heart. For whatever I give you to do I will also fill you with the grace and strength to do it. I know that you have many worldly things to do, but is it not important to spread the good news from our Heavenly Father? Remember the harvest is ready but the workers are few. Begin with the few workers that are ready. Perhaps others will see their harvest and join them. Fire spreads fast. Water spreads fast. It is time for God's word to spread fast bringing many to the Shepherd becoming part of His flock so that the workers will be many.

09/20/11 (time unknown)

Now My children now you know how it is to live in Satan's world. A world of selfishness. A world of hate. A world without true love. Everyone always looking for My promise and it is right in front of you. Many search technology for love. Did you not read My word? I created woman and man with My own hands. Why are you looking for a partner on the computer? My people are you so shallow that you cannot go out into the world and greet and meet a companion? Must you over load others with how wonderful you are? Can't others see that you glow with faith, hope, and love? If it is there it will glow. If it is not there you can find it in My word. Seek ye first the kingdom of God and all of these things (including your companion) will be yours. My children use your light to cover the world with a glow of love and peace. And then I will say thank you My good and faithful servant. I love you. I AM.

09/25/11 (12:50 a.m.)

My darling daughters how I rejoice in seeing each of you reading your text and especially your venture in exploring the Bible. Many women followed Me. Often it is difficult to understand. Whenever you're not sure about something you've read just walk away from it awhile. Soon you will know Me better. Do you know how you're being challenged with your group? Did you know that you need to share with everyone especially the poor. This is not just sharing food and clothing, it is also sharing food and money. You don't have to figure out where to go. Need is all around. Some need money, others need shelter, and others may need medicine. There are many broken hearts, worn out patience, and low self-esteem. You must touch each heart and lift them up to Me. Yes your heart can be sent to Me also. I will heal them and fill them with an abundance of love, peace, and joy. Come My daughters it is time for you to receive all of Me and reap all that I have promised.

09/28/11 (3:45 a.m.)

Listen to the words that I speak. Many of you listen to My messenger. You rejoice and praise and then you leave the building and leave what the messenger has delivered behind in the church. You do not come to be sprinkled with good news, but rather bombarded and over loaded with My word. Your heart is pounding with news to share with all you come in contact with. Listen, it is good that you come to be fueled and refueled, but it has to go further. You've got to tell somebody. Or at least take it another step deeper with someone that received the same word. Please don't walk out without stretching it out to others or deepening it with a member. Church, the message must go on and on and on. Do you not feel the fire in your heart? Water is not passed around to extinguish that fire because it's supposed to burn in you to deliver to others until I, the Lord God Almighty, cool the coals. It is then that you can rest from sharing the message given to you. It is then when I will say well done My good and faithful servant. Well done.

11/15/11 (5:15 a.m.)

My Darling Daughters of Zion: know that I am with you. I am with you to maintain peace, joy, and wisdom within you. It is within you because I planted those seeds the moment you began seeking Me. Know that each step you took toward getting to know more of My word those seeds grew. Just think of it within your mind, your heart, and your soul there is a garden. Whenever things of this world disturb you just go within and gather the peace that you need. Whenever the worldly things have caused you sadness, go within and gather so much joy that it causes your smile to be like a beacon of light to others. Whenever you become confused as to which way to go or with any choices you need to make, then go within and gather wisdom that will lead you in the right direction and make the right choices for you. Know that I am with you nurturing your garden as you absorb My word. Read My word. Listen to My word. Sing My word. Sing praises to Me. Do these things and you will never be without your garden that flourishes with the peace, joy, and wisdom that you need. Listen to My word daughters of Zion. Read them and listen with your heart. Know that you have not heard truer words. When things are not right in your life, follow these directions. Know that I am your Father. Know that I love you forever. Know that I AM.

Date Unknown

My children: I know that many of you have grown
weary waiting for My word to rescue you from whatever
discomfort you are in. It is there for you at all times. You
need but read My word, open your heart to it, let your
mind conceive, and it will be done. When? You ask.
Well it could be as soon as you accept it fully without
a doubt in your heart. You see My little one, I am your
Father. I want you to trust in Me as much as you desire
for Me to trust in you. However, you know how far that
goes. You spend a little time waiting and then turn to
some kind of entertainment of the world. You lose faith
and believe that the good and comfort and healing will
probably come at the end of time. But My children
you must not lose faith for what I have promised is for
you here on earth. It is like reading a good book. You
anxiously read waiting for the best part and then what
great satisfaction. Then you are rewarded with what

you'd hoped for. My word (the Bible) is the same. You must continue to read it until you learn how to cast out all that is not from Me. Continue to read My word until My promises are embedded in your heart and then they will unfold before you. It is like a candy store. Take as many graces as you need. Fill yourself with love, peace, and joy. Don't forget to get all of the healings that you need. I am your Father. I have stored many good things for you. All I want is for you to know My word and make it a part of your thought process and every beat of your heart. Eye hath not seen nor ear heard of the wonders and riches that I have stored for you. Come My little ones. Come and seek and be filled abundantly. I love you and desire to pour all of My riches upon you. I AM.

11/17/11 (12:30 a.m.)

My children know that I am with you. Listen and you will hear Me speak to you. Listen and you will hear Me cheer you on in all you do. Listen and you will hear Me call you to an even more divine ministry. Yes My child I am always trying to get your attention. There is always something for you to do. It may be something to help you or another grow spiritually or just to be still and feel My presence and know that I am God. As God your heavenly Father I will catch you when you fall and set you high. Know that I have come to give you life more abundantly. Stop asking when, when, when. Just know with all of your heart that I the Father will bring about a better day for you that hear Me; so that you can help others to hear and bring about a better day for them. How can you hear Me you ask? I've told you that. You simply have to open your heart as you read My Holy word and you will hear Me right within your heart. As you read the words again, you will understand them better. You will know how to obtain the many gifts that the disciples had. You must know that Jesus loves you as much as He loved the disciples. I am waiting to send you out to heal and anoint others. It is My desire to have all around Me filled with the Holy Spirit to give to all of those being led to God's kingdom. Listen to Me My children. The harvest is ready but the labors are few. I need you to be a light to the perfect light. Bring My sheep home. I AM.

03/03/12 (1:10 a.m.)

My little ones I know that the road to salvation is lonely. There are many that busy themselves with the ways of the world filled with criticism of others and without even love of self. How can we love others as ourselves when we do not even love ourselves? Are you taking care of your temple that is the dwelling place for the Holy Spirit? Is that temple well-nourished with the fruits of the earth, My word, and hydrated? Does your temple glorify Me with a peaceful, joyful, loving disposition at all times? I have made you in My image. Should you not reflect My goodness? Make every effort to do so. When you feel you can't, come aside awhile to be refreshed and refueled. I am always with you and prepared to fulfill your every need in Jesus name. I AM.

03/07/12 (1:10 a.m.)

Though you wrestle with the angel that I have sent during the night, you do not hear Me calling you. I have sent My angel many times. You wrestle and refuse to rise. You cannot sleep and you will not rise to talk to Me. All I want to do is to assure you of My constant presence. I feel your loneliness and your sadness because of it. My child, you are not alone. I have called you at this early hour so that you can hear Me in the quiet stillness. There are no sounds to drown out. Now listen, really listen. I love you. I need you to feel My love wrapped around you. I want you to feel My love filling your heart. Now filled and covered with My love you have no doubt of My love for you. You have so much. You need to give much of it away. Go right ahead and start giving it away. Have you noticed no matter how much you give away, you are still filled and covered as in the beginning? And even better the more you give away the more you have. That's right I want to give much to you; much love, much peace, much joy, much healing, much prosperity, and many spiritual gifts so that you can give them away. Your life will be fulfilled. And I will say well done My good and faithful servant. With you I am well pleased. I AM.

03/15/12 (12:55 a.m.)

Why do you worry? Have I not shown you how tenderly I provide for the sparrow, how lovely the lilies are clothed, and how they neither worry nor toil? These things are before you and yet you fret. Have you not read that you are even more than the sparrow and the lilies of the fields? So shouldn't you know that you will be fed and clothed? Trust your Heavenly Father for all things. Whether it is food, shelter, clothing, healing, peace, joy, or love. I am your Father and I will provide it for you. Actually it's all here for you right now. Open the door to your heart and I will enter. I'll fill your inner spirit with all that you need. And behold your body has been covered with the most beautiful clothing eyes have ever seen. Behold yourself! You are beautiful, healthy, and filled with God's loving peace and joy. So be not afraid. Trust in Me the Lord God Almighty and you will receive beyond your wildest dream because I love you and feel your love for Me.

03/21/12 (4:25 a.m.)

My beloved children yes I call you My children for no matter how old you may be you will always be My child/ My children. I will always be your Father. I will always be your provider. No, you never out grow the things that you need from Me. For the things that cometh from Me cannot be obtained on earth nor from your earthly parents. I, your Heavenly Father, am ready to give you peace of mind and heart. This peace that cometh from Me surpasses the understanding of mankind. I am ready to give you joy. That joy will remain with you through all challenges and disappointments. I am ready to send you provisions for you and your love ones. Yes, I will prepare a table before you in the presence of your enemies (those that say you cannot provide for yourself and family). I am ready to renew your strength and heal your body. That is heal every muscle, bone, joint, and organ. Why do I keep saying that I am ready to do all these things?

Well My children I am ready. I'm only waiting for you to acknowledge and believe that you can receive these things from Me and only Me. Then open your heart and all of these blessings will be poured upon you. Your cup will run over to others willing to believe and receive. I love you My children. I love you and I wait for you to receive Me fully. I AM.

03/28/12 (4:35 a.m.)

And lo, I am with you. I am with you every moment of your life. If you do not hear Me it is because you are not listening for Me. If you do not feel Me, it's because you have shut Me out. I am always seeking your attention and your permission to step in and heal you, guide you, provide for you, and protect you from the shadow of darkness. How can you read My word and think that I, your Heavenly Father, would leave and forsake you? I, even more than your earthly father love you. I have carved you from the palm of My hand. Can you even imagine that in flesh? I have prepared the way for you. You only have to choose to follow it to all you will ever need to remain happy forever after. There are no earthly words to explain the love that I have for you. Yes you! I know that you have found fault with yourself. But that is because you look to others for self worth. Look unto the heavens. Look unto your creator for I know every atom of your being. I am more than pleased with what I have created. You are a master piece. You are worthy. I hold you in the palm of My hand for I am your Heavenly Father and with you I am well pleased.

04/11/12 (3:20 a.m.)

You say that you know who I am but do you really know Me? Do you know that I have created all things? Just look about you. See the stars, the sky, the trees, the birds, the rain, the sun, the mountains, the sea, and as far as you can see in every direction I have created it. Even those things built by man, I have given them the design and method of creating the images of their mind. I heal and give peace to all who seek Me. Seek Me more and open yourself to the healing, love, peace, and joy that I have prepared for you. Seek not and you have not. For who can deliver pass a closed door? Well you say to God, which I am, all things are possible. Yes, I can do all things, but I will not deliver beyond a closed door. However I will keep these gifts and much more at your threshold just waiting for you to say come Lord Jesus into my heart which I open to you. No matter how long it takes I will rejoice when that time comes. I, the creator of all things in heaven and earth and beyond desire to dwell in your heart, fill you with My Holy Spirit and use you to heal, love, and comfort My people. I desire to set you on fire with My love so that you will be a light to the perfect light and warm all of the cold hearts on earth. Yes, even those in the churches that pour out words so eloquently need to warm their cold hearts. I love all of My children. My greatest desire is that you love Me with all of your heart, mind, and soul and love your neighbor as yourself. Don't forget to love yourself My little ones. My love for you is everlasting. I AM.

05/08/12 (1:00 a.m.)

Listen to the words I speak. How many ways have I told you that I am here for you? How many times have I told you that I am here for you? With you I am well pleased. You think you have not done enough? Well you have. You have led them to the perfect light. You have opened your soul unto them. Some follow you to Me. Some are so lost they may never be found. Share your peaceful manner, your love, and your joy in spirit. All of these things cometh from Me. I have more for all that come to Me. I love My children of the earth. I hope that they love and respect Me. That is not much to ask. Pray for those that call on My name and use foul words. Do not put one foot in My door and keep one in the world. Come to Me completely rejoicing and praising God. And then I will pour My gifts upon you. Eye hath not seen nor ear heard what I have prepared for each one of you. Rejoice and come to My house. I love you. I AM.

04/19/13 (12:30 a.m.)

My children I have called you here to listen to My word. These are words of gladness, of love, of peace, and of prosperity. Know that I, the Father of all, understand all of your needs. I know the loneliness in your heart even though you are with a spouse. I know of your financial lack. I know what will give you joy and fill your heart with gladness. All of this can be accomplished by opening your heart and let Me come in. I am the healer of all brokenness. Have you not heard that I have raised the dead? Can you even imagine how much power that must take? There is no hopelessness with Me. Believe in Me. Hope in Me. Have faith in Me. I love you. I will never forsake you. Do not give up on the desires of your heart. Do not insist on fixing things yourself. Give it all to Me. I am your Father in whom all things are possible. Give it to Me. Rest in Me. Believe in Me and My love for you. I AM.

4/30/13 (11:30 p.m.)

What do you hear in the night? Is it the sound of My voice or another? I call you to peace and love everlasting. I call you to joy in great abundance. I call you to come unto Me, to listen to My word, to learn about Me, and to know Me fully. I call you to know yourself and love yourself. Truly I have created a thing of beauty in you. Can you hear Me calling you over and over again? I will not give up. I will continue to whisper your name until you give Me your listening ear. I have so much to give you. I hold out to you healing of your body, mind, and soul. I hold out to you the grace of forgiveness. I hold out to you the peace that surpasses all mankind. Can you even imagine that? Come My little one. Come sit upon your Father's knee. Come apart from the world and spend time with Me. I am your Father. I created you to love. Come.

05/23/13 (12:38 a.m.)

To those of you who wish to spend more time with Me, draw closer to Me, and hear My every word; I call you to do just that. Put aside the concerns of the world and just spend time with Me. Allow your heart and soul to absorb My written word and words spoken by those that I have sent you. For truly these are My promises to you and everyone who has come with you. Know that I am Lord of all power and that My deepest desire is to please you with an abundance of heavenly blessings. Can you not comprehend that? My love for you is like none other on the face of the earth. My love for you is passionate, gentle, enduring, safe, and forever. Close your eyes and just imagine and absorb the love that I give to you. It is more than the mind can contain. There are no earthly words to express the intensity of My love for you. Rest in it. Walk in it. Sleep in it. Believe in it with all of your heart. I give you all of My love. As you walk toward Me you absorb more and more of it. Soak in it. Share it. Share it. My little one share it with all you meet. I love you.

05/25/13 (12:45 a.m.)

My little ones I call you My little ones because forever you are My children. Forever I will hold you in the palm of My hand. Forever I will walk with you. When you are not able to walk I will carry you. Forever I will whisper I love you in your ear. Forever I will long for you to hear those words of love and so much more. I actually do walk and talk with you but you fail to listen. I have healed your body, your heart, and yes even your mind but it all goes unnoticed. Is it because these things do not appear brand new as though when your life begun? Oh My little one renewing keeps you going and enlightens your spirit. Be not sad because your body is not like the days of your youth. But rather be happy and at peace for the strength and peace of mind that you have. Be thankful for the wisdom that you have. Be thankful for the grace to forgive unconditionally. Be content with your physical changes. For as sure as your movement becomes slower, your mind has become more peaceful and your spirit closer to Me as it should be. Continue to grow into Me and allow Me to be a greater part of you until there is no longer you or Me but just one. I love you My little one. Forever I love you.

05/26/13 (12:10 a.m.)

The dawn comes and a new day has begun. Do you know what this day has in store for you? Is it love, peace, and joy? Or is it tragedy and sadness? It matters not what awaits you, but rather how prepared you are. Have you allowed Me to enter your heart? If so we will face all things together. And the peace that surpasses the understanding of all mankind will be with you no matter what. Facing challenges without Me will cause depression, loneliness, and thoughts leading to suicide. Trust in Me My child. Simply say yes I accept Jesus Christ as my Lord and Savior and we are one. Now is the time, the acceptable moment. Say yes. Open the door to your heart. Just invite Me in and we are one forever. I AM.

05/27/13 (12:40 a.m.)

There is more, much more for all of God's children. Did I not say that I have come to give you life more abundantly? Do not merely cast your eyes upon material things. Think about the greater gifts of the spirit. Isn't joy a great gift? Doesn't it lift you up from a sad encounter? Think of peace. Isn't it wonderful to be at peace without the use of the drugs that the world turns to? My peace passes the understanding of all mankind. Think of love. Not as the world speaks of love, here today and gone tomorrow; conditional and unforgiving. My love is everlasting. My love is passionate. My love is forgiving. My love encourages you to do good for others. My love has no fear but rather rebukes evil. My love is with you at all times. It never turns away from you. Come and soak in My love. My love is for you. I AM

05/28/13 (12:45a.m.)

Love them for Me. You must love them for Me. There are many among you that need to know My love. They need to know that My love is pure. There is no sin connected to My love. My love is warm and safe. There is no fear with My love. My love is for all of those seeking Me. How can you give My love, you ask? My love feeds the poor. My love provides shelter for the homeless. My love clothes those without clothes. My love lifts the spirit of the down hearted. My love is a companion for the lonely. Won't you be My love to one of My children in need? I do not call you to be all things for all of My children because My body has many branches. Reach out and share My love with one or more at a time. Love them. Love them. Love them for Me. As you give you will begin to feel drained. Fear not I await to renew and refuel you. Your reward is great both in heaven and on earth. The highest and deepest gratification is when you hear Me say well done My good and faithful servant. With you I am well pleased. I love you. My love for you surpasses the understanding of all mankind. I AM

Glory

be to

GOD

Forever!

Printed in the United States
By Bookmasters